PERMISSION

A Guide to Generating More Ideas
Being More of Yourself
and Having More Fun at Work

ISBN: 0615529224
ISBN-13: 978-0615529226

PERMISSION

A Guide to Generating More Ideas
Being More of Yourself
and Having More Fun at Work

co-created by
Pamela Meyer & Brandy Agerbeck

Playspace
Press

Permission: An Introduction

This is a playful book with serious intent. Here's the serious part: Most individuals and organizations espouse wonderful ideals. They advocate for innovation, questioning old assumptions, change, flexibility, responsiveness, empowerment, engagement, and leadership. Making these ideals a reality is something else entirely. In Pamela Meyer's research on innovative organizations and the space people create for innovating, learning, and changing, she made a new discovery: While people may have an intellectual understanding of the espoused values of organizational innovation, learning, and change, the people who actually innovate, learn, and enact change each day get, take, and most important—*give* permission to do so.

The permission-giver is one of the most important roles anyone can play to encourage innovative thinking, significant learning, and engagement at work.

1

Most people need to be given permission for innovating, learning, and changing (among other positive behaviors) even when the words inscribed on the vision and values statement in the lobby or company website invite them to do just that. Most of us are trained to take our cues from the environment itself. Despite explicit messages of the organization's values, we are more attuned to implicit rules and expectations. A promising new hire will scan the environment to get a sense of the accepted norms for behavior, dress (jeans and flip-flops or suit and tie?), hours (flexible or fixed?), chain of communication (open or hierarchal?), and more. This promising new hire in the first few days on the job may hang back a bit in meetings and conversations as she learns about the projects, personalities, and expectations related to her role. If she notices that junior people don't tend to speak up in meetings, she may get the message that, despite the lip service being paid, the ideas of junior employees are not welcome. Rather than risk making a bad impression right out of the gate, she avoids testing the perceived norm, thus reinforcing and, in fact, making her perception reality, as many who have gone before her have done. The same process can be recreated by long-term employees as they settle into the comfort of the culture and climate of the organization. New ideas, perspectives, and insight can be disruptive. Why stir things up when you can relax into the tried and true?

There are, of course, few if any sectors that have the luxury of counting on "the way we've always done things around here" to sustain their success, let alone growth. Not long ago, government agencies such as the U.S. Postal Service were called out as rare exceptions; not any more. All who care about their continued success now need to take responsibility for giving, taking, and getting permission for ongoing innovating, learning, and changing if they are to survive and thrive. All of this is in the interest of much more than these high-level organizational imperatives—it is in the interest of your everyday experience at work. By giving yourself and others permission to bring their whole selves, great ideas, and fresh perspectives to each conversation and collaboration, you will find the whole endeavor much more engaging and, well...simply more fun!

Three Ways to Break Through Numbing Organizational Routine

The creativity, insights, and positive energy lost in prevailing workplace norms and routines can be regained by three simple practices, give permission, take permission, get permission. The great news is that each of these can be practiced by anyone at any level of your organization.

Give Permission

Giving permission means putting your organizational ideals and espoused values into practice every day. It is much more that giving lip service; it means actually behaving *in service* of your values. Being a permission-giver also means living into your aspirational vision of what you want your organization, and your life within it, to look and feel like. If you wish your organization were a little more creative, playful, and fun, then you will want to be sure that you are giving others permission to create, play, and have fun through your own behavior, attitude, and demeanor.

Most of us have been well trained to follow the rules. It doesn't take long to scope out the environment and get a sense of what the rules are in any workplace. Even the most enthusiastic and creative among us sometimes need encouragement and permission to step out of the perceived norms, stretch others' thinking, challenge cherished assumptions, and just plain play around a little bit.

Those who understand the importance of permission-giving know that telling someone they have permission is much less effective than actually modeling the permitted behavior. Actions really do speak louder than words. For this reason, many of the ideas in the book are action-oriented and are presented with the understanding that to truly be a permission-giver, you must first *take* permission.

Take Permission

Visionaries and pioneers throughout history have not waited around to understand the rules and wait for permission to break them; they jump right in and take permission from whatever real or imagined authorities exist at the moment. Permission-takers enthusiastically lead the way, risk being called names, and generally clear the path for those of us who are a bit too timid to be the very first to try something new. While it is rarely their main mission, permission-takers also *give* others permission to live into their best selves, too, and to work (and play) at the top of their talent by giving us a glimpse of what is possible. Thanks to the permission-takers in the world, more people now know it really is okay to speak up in meetings, be a little silly, take a break, challenge sacred cows, and much more.

Get Permission

One of us (Pamela) first noticed the phenomenon of permission-getting while researching peoples' experiences learning improvisation. Something interesting happened each quarter after she took her adult students on a field trip to a local improv club. As they watched in awe and delight as their much more experienced counterparts created an entire evening of theater based on one or two suggestions from the audience, something started to shift. By the time everyone met back in the classroom the following week, most reported feeling more confident and open to experimenting. By witnessing the boundary-pushing play in the improv club, they *got* permission to push beyond their own preconceived boundaries.

This form of permission-getting is passive and often unexpected. Just a few ways we can get permission are by watching a colleague jump up in the middle of a meeting and passionately defend his idea, by encountering a completely new approach to an issue or challenge that has stumped us, or being exposed to an entirely fresh way of doing things.

The true power of permission-getting comes when we take responsibility for actively seeking out permission.

The most successful permission-getters do not leave inspiration to chance: they are intentional and explicit in their search. Some of the most effective innovators actively seek out provocative examples to give them permission to push beyond their own ideas and preconceptions. Permission-getters go on field trips to visit other businesses and industries, they talk with innovators and boundary-pushers in their own and other fields, they attend and present at conferences (often in other areas than their own). Permission-getters regularly seek examples and ideas on the Internet, watch inspiring videos, talks and slide presentations, read provocative books, and consume a wide range of media. Permission-getters know the value of looking beyond the comfort of their own domain for fresh perspectives, ideas, and inspiration.

Playing the Role of Permission-Giver, -Taker, and -Getter

Permission-givers, -takers, and -getters create *playspace**. Playspace is a mindset shift and a way of being more than an actual space. In playspace the very concept of play (long-banned from the workplace) is reclaimed as a key dynamic of success. In this reclaimed space there is room for the *play* of new ideas and perspectives, for people to *play* new roles and develop new capacities, for more *play* in the system, and for improvised *play*. Permission-givers who consciously and enthusiastically play their role, in turn, have the biggest impact on the play*ing* space.

Taking on the role of permission-giver is quite simple and requires only a few commitments to do intentionally and in the spirit of creating more space for all to work (and play) at the top of their talent.

Six Principles of Permission

 Create Safe Space. The biggest barrier to sharing new ideas (i.e., sharing more of ourselves) as well as innovating, learning, and changing, is the fear of repercussions. For most, the biggest risk is not physical, or even financial; it is the risk of losing credibility, appearing stupid, or looking foolish. For this reason, one of the most

---

* Meyer, Pamela. 2010. *From Workplace to Playspace: Innovating, Learning and Changing Through Dynamic Engagement*. San Francisco: Jossey-Bass.

important responsibilities of the permission-giver is his or her ability to make the space safe enough for people to risk showing up in new and sometimes unfamiliar ways. Keeping the following principles in mind will go a long way toward creating safe space.

Model it Yourself. You can't give others permission for anything you are not doing yourself. To model permission you might first need to play the role of a permission-taker before you can be a permission-giver. Depending on your role, you may not be able to model the permission exactly (e.g., the way a computer programmer gives permission for innovating may look very different from how a bank manager does). More important than *how* you model any given permission is *that* you model it. The spirit of your good intentions goes a long way when it comes to permission-giving.

Be You. Bring your whole imperfect self to permission-giving. Going through the motions of a permission is just as meaningless (and even detrimental) as only giving lip service. It is just fine to voice your discomfort, or even announce that you feel a little silly sharing something or playing a new role as you dive into it; it will only make you all the more human and your permission all the more compelling to your fellow players.

Play Within the Givens. Another common misgiving about boldly giving, taking, and getting permission is that you might cross a non-negotiable boundary. Such transgressions in certain highly-regulated or high-risk industries could be disastrous. Permission-givers are responsible for setting people up for success by being clear about those non-negotiable boundaries. Just as stage improvisers play freely within the givens established by audience suggestions or their fellow players, be sure *your* fellow players understand their givens, and then lead the way in showing what it might look like to play within them!

Get Over Yourself. The risk of giving, getting, or taking a new permission diminishes greatly when you take the focus off of yourself and put it on your fellow players. Rather than worry if you are going to look silly by being the first to express your enthusiasm for a new initiative, or sharing a fresh new idea, put your attention (and intention) on supporting the success of the group, the organization, your mission, customers, etc. When you give, take, or get permission in service of something larger than yourself, the pressure to maintain some mythical (and static) identity eases.

Don't Take It Too Seriously. As soon as permission-giving becomes another strategic initiative or item on your to-do list, it loses its essential life energy. Seriousness and "purpose" are the death of permission-giving. This is a bit paradoxical, as is our claim that this is a playful book with a serious intent. If you approach your permission-giving, -taking and -getting with a playful spirit, the serious intent will take care of itself. So Keep It Simple Sweetie and have fun!

How to Use This Book for Optimum Permission

Read It Through Once. To enjoy the full spectrum of permissions, and perhaps be reminded of a few you had forgotten, we recommend reading the entire book through once. While we arranged the permissions in an order that made some sense to us, we are not attached to it. You may enjoy reading the permissions from back to front, or the middle out, or any other order that suits you. The most important thing is that you don't miss that one permission that could change your life!

Play Permission Tarot. Once you've gotten an overview, keep your copy of *Permission* within reach and regularly flip it open to a random page. Chances are you will get exactly the permission you (and perhaps your colleagues) need at the moment.

Give It Away. We intentionally crafted this book for maximum share-ability. In addition to your personal use, it is meant for gifting, sharing, and borrowing.

You may want to give away the entire book, or a single permission by bookmarking a page and leaving it on the desk of your friend, colleague, boss, co-worker, partner, or other anyone else. Visit www.permissiongivers.com for more fun ideas for "who to" and "how to" give permission.

Finally, Give, Take, and Get Permission. It is all too easy to slip into thinking it is everyone *else* who needs to take permission and to forget about taking responsibility for our own role. When we truly value the things that can happen when people have permission—fresh ideas, exciting new connections, innovation, learning, and positive change, as well as engagement, fun, and outright joy—we take seriously our role and responsibility to give, take, and get permission.

Congratulations!

We now officially give you permission to give permission.

Permission to
Listen to Your
Whole Body

Many of us live most of our waking hours from the neck up. Our disembodied selves tap, tap, tap away on the keyboard, participate in meetings and conference calls, and rarely remember that we are whole people living in whole bodies.

The liability of leaving our body behind is that we can lose important information, insight, and energy that live in our bodies. Insight, intuition, "gut feelings," and inspiration often bubble up from beyond our rational selves. Our bodies and all of our senses also tell us when we've had enough, when we need to rest, when we need to move, dive in, and so much more.

Permission to
Listen to Your Whole Body

Monitor the Inputs

We have five (some say more) senses for a reason! Taking time throughout the day to notice what you are experiencing will give you important information. Are you always exhausted after meeting about X project or working with Y colleague? What needs to shift? Are you hungry and crabby every day at the same time? How can you take care of yourself? Does your heart flutter with excitement whenever you talk about your new learning? How can you nurture that passion?

Ask for a Gut Check

It is common to ask colleagues and collaborators what they *think*. Give yourself permission to regularly ask yourself and everyone else what they *feel*. You may be surprised at the information available when everyone is given permission to listen to their whole bodies.

Notice and Name It

Sometimes new insight is as simple as naming what we are experiencing. Take permission to simply notice and name what you are experiencing at any given moment. In time, you will become more attuned to the wealth of information available from your whole body and be even more responsive, creative, engaged, and (let's face it) awesome than you already are!

Permission to Change Your P.O.V.

Every great story has a point of view. Storytellers, visionary thinkers, and leaders inspire and challenge us with their perspectives. Those who are true innovators are also not afraid to *change* their point of view from time to time. Sometimes they even play around with new perspectives for fun, just to see what the world might look like if viewed from another direction.

Changing your P.O.V. can take some doing, even some courage. First, of course, you need to be aware that you *have* a point of view. This view might have taken hold early in your life or emerged later as you were exposed to more ways of thinking and being. Regardless of when and how it came to be, you are likely pretty darn comfortable with it by now. You may even have a network of like-minded folks who share your P.O.V. and have a stake in your perspective staying Just. As. It. Is.

That is a lot of pressure. Unless, of course, we all lighten up and take permission to change our point of view, even for a few minutes, just for fun, just to see what we see from over   here.

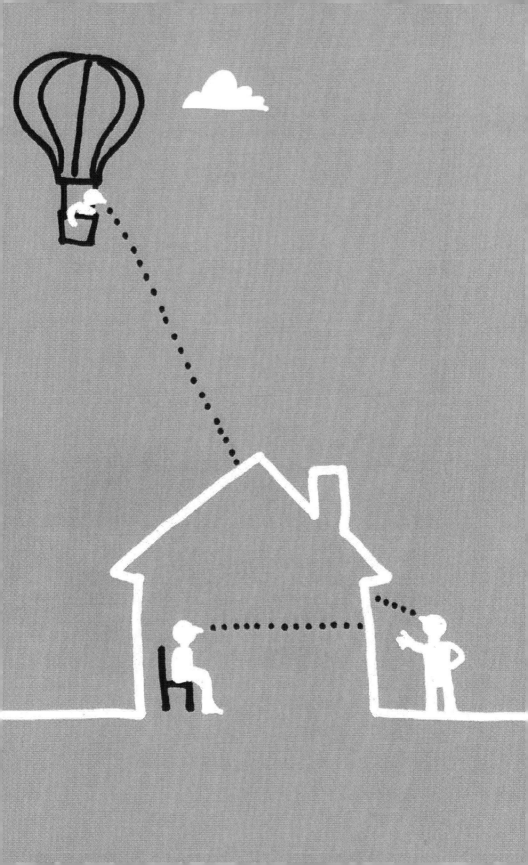

Permission to
Change Your P.O.V.

Move Closer, Move Farther

Sometimes our perspective is measured in distance. Maybe you are too close to the matter at hand, or too far away. Perhaps you need to get out your binoculars or magnifying glass to look at the finer details. Maybe you need to step back or look through the other end of your telescope to see the bigger picture. What have you been missing simply because you were using a lens that limited your view?

Get a Second Opinion

Seek out the contrarians, the people who hail from another part of the forest and see the world completely different than you do. The best time to get a second opinion is not necessarily when you are not getting the news you hoped for; get a second opinion when everyone is cheering you on and telling you how great you/your idea is. Have you missed any input that might make you/your idea even better than it is? You'll never know unless you ask.

Step into Another Person's Shoes

Job sharing and shadowing are popular practices to give people new perspectives in the workplace. What would happen if you shadowed or shared outside of your familiar domain? What other perspectives might open up? Especially if you can immerse yourself in the world of those who hold the views furthest from your own. How are they making sense of the world? What media, support system, and social networks reinforce their P.O.V.? Step into their shoes; you don't even have to walk an entire mile. Even a few blocks may be enough to jiggle things around a bit.

Permission to Be Silly

Quick. Make a face.

Crinkle or contort the one you usually wear. What happens? Making a face is a wonderful release. If you happen to make your face with an audience, you are sure to get a response. Face-making, sound-making, hat-wearing, bubble-blowing, wiggle-worming, word-playing, and all forms of general goofiness create space—welcome space.

Silliness is best engaged in spontaneously and without purpose or direction.

Perhaps most important, silliness shifts the group energy and gives others permission to settle down, settle in, and bring their whole wonderful (and silly) selves into the mix. The release you felt in your face will wash through your whole body and others' bodies, and soon people will be playing with new ideas, roles, and possibilities.

Permission to
Be Silly

Assemble Your Silly Posse

Think about it. Who do you allow yourself to be silliest with? Likely it is with people whom you have no fear of judgment and who will fully appreciate your silly energy and hopefully even join in to support your shenanigans. Your silly posse might start with just you, but soon you will attract at least one other playmate to keep the good times rolling. Before long you may find yourself taking permission to be silly without your posse anywhere in sight—to the delight of anyone who happens to be in your good energy.

Create the Context

In what contexts or settings do you allow your silliness to come out and play? Most of us need some gentle mix of safety and relaxation plus permission not to take ourselves too seriously. One sure sign that people feel safe is when we start to see their silly side. Notice what space you have created that allows for silliness and celebrate all who contribute to it.

Take the Lead

Don't wait around for someone to give you permission for some silly-time. If everyone waited for someone else to take the lead, we'd never have any silliness (or the playspace for new ideas and engagement it ignites) at all! What if the leader they are waiting for is *you*? What if the time is *now*?

Permission to
Incubate

Most things worth waiting for need time to incubate, gestate, take shape, and emerge. Living things and great ideas all need to incubate. The pressure to produce may beckon you to truncate, force, or skip this stage. If you have ever tried to rush a relationship, a still forming opportunity, or the tomato plant on your patio, you know just how fruitless this is. Why not accept and appreciate the natural process of life and give yourself (and other living things) permission to incubate?

Permission to
Incubate

Give It Time

All living things and generative processes have their own internal timeline. Perhaps we don't give *it* time so much as we need to give *ourselves* time to be present and appropriately participatory during the incubation. Some processes need quiet monitoring under the proverbial grow light, while others benefit from lively engagement in several rounds of imaginative conversations. All require patience and time.

Appreciate Emergence

Appreciating emergence means actively valuing the process of becoming. When we appreciate unfolding itself, we are much more mindful custodians of the process (not just the product) and tend to be nicer to each other along the way, too!

Give It Space

Many baby chicks come into the world in climate-controlled hatcheries, and humans are swaddled in nurseries (as are, interestingly, fledgling plants and trees). Each of these spaces is thoughtfully, lovingly attended to for the sole purpose of supporting growth. What kind of space is required to incubate the growth of your emerging _____ (fill-in-the-blank)? What would happen if you attended to that space with the care of a new mother or master arborist?

Permission to
Iterate

Iteration is the stuff of innovation, continuous improvement, and learning. The obstacle to iteration is also the obstacle to progress: an attachment to our ideas and perspectives. When you release this attachment and give yourself permission to iterate, amazing new possibilities open up. Take a lesson from software developers: the 2.0 version will be even more user-friendly than the 1.0, and look out for the 2.1 iteration—it will really knock your socks off!

Giving and taking permission to iterate has another benefit. Iteration invites a mindset shift from striving for the perfect product, service, or creation, to attending to the process itself. Valuing the process as much as the product means attending to the space for creating, communicating, and collaborating. Attending to the verbs (process) will yield even more wonderful nouns (products).

Permission to
Iterate

Look for the Second, Third, and Fourth Answer

Many of us are still recovering from our traditional educations that rewarded us for getting the right answer rather than for the questions we asked. Part of our recovery program requires not stopping at the first answer to the question, but looking for the second, third, and fourth answers and beyond!

Shop It Around

One of the best ways to get fuel for your next iteration is to shop your *last* iteration around. Think of your idea as a prototype that needs to be tested and played with. Listen carefully to the feedback (the authentic user experience)—especially the input that you are most tempted to dismiss.

Experiment

With a scientist's commitment, ask your question, form your hypothesis, conduct your experiment, analyze the data, discuss and contemplate the results, and begin the cycle again. In experimentation there are no mistakes, only results. With a little humility, an attitude of inquiry, and the passion of a mad scientist, you will head back into your laboratory again and again.

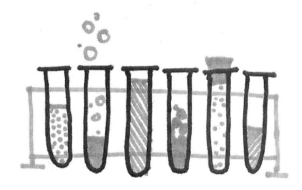

Permission to
Move

With all of the trend talk about our increasingly mobile workforce, most of us are remarkably immobile in our daily lives. Just as we often miss important information available to us when we are disconnected from our whole bodies, we can lose the fluidity of energy and perspectives when we get overly stationary physically and/or conceptually.

Permission to move, then, is literally permission to move your body in time and space throughout the day (first you must remember you have a body!) and it is also permission to move your familiar ways of thinking, being, and perceiving. Not surprisingly, when we give ourselves permission to move our bodies, our ideas often start moving, too!

Permission to
Move

Reclaim Recess

Have you been sitting too long? Working on the same project without a break? Reclaim what used to be one of the best parts of the school day—a few minutes to play! It can be a literal game (solo or group), a jaunt around the block, or even a quick round of chair yoga—anything to get your blood flowing and refresh your energy and perspective.

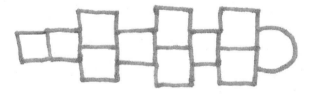

Stand It Up

Some of the best meetings occur in short bursts as people gather on their feet for updates, or to share exciting ideas and developments. You can also stand up during your phone conversations. Give yourself permission to animate your sales call or next conference call by standing and moving your body while you talk and listen.

Dance, Wiggle, Bounce

It's so simple. A few minutes of music (turn the lights out if you are shy) and permission to dance, wiggle, and/or bounce will do amazing things to bring the energy back into the room and everyone back into their bodies. Welcome home!

Permission to Be Human

It's a lot, being human. None of us remember being tipped off to just how *much* it would be, or how much it would take. Showing up to the big and small events, challenges, and surprises of adult life is a lot. Showing up to all of our internal changes and transformations as we grow, accumulate experience (and occasionally wisdom), and mature takes even more. We can't be expected to show up and move through all of this like a well-tuned machine or with endless grace and detachment. We can only be expected to be human—that is, if we give ourselves permission to be. Being human means being whole, authentic, and, yes, sometimes even messy.

Permission to
Be Human

Practice Self-Compassion

Financial advisors often recommend that we "pay ourselves first" when managing our resources. This is good counsel when it comes to compassion, too. It is a wonderful goal to be more compassionate toward others *and* in pursuit of that goal, we easily leapfrog over the person most in need of it—ourselves. Are you frustrated that you were short with a colleague? Negative in a meeting? Impatient with your fellow commuters? How can you be more compassionate toward *yourself* today? Once you discover the answer, you will be able to extend a bit of that compassion to others.

Breeeeeeeeathe

Ah...doesn't that feel good? Humans breathe. Every day, all day long. When we steel ourselves against the chaos, stress, and uncertainty around us, we start holding our breath.

Let it go.   Right now.   Breeeeeeeeathe.

There, doesn't that feel better?

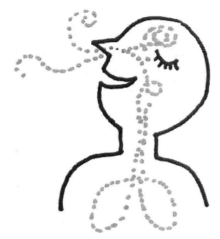

Let it Out

Being human means letting out more than just our breath. It sometimes means letting some sound ride on the wave of that breath. If you can muster it, try it now.

Big.   Long.   Loud.   Sigh.

What else might you let out with that sigh? What emotions might you give yourself permission to express? Sometimes expressing emotions is for our own internal healing and integration. Sometimes we need to give ourselves permission to express emotions in the moment and let our humanity out. Experiencing and expressing emotions are essential parts of being human and natural responses to all you are showing up to and responsible for. There is information, insight, and power in those emotions.

Breathe into it, with compassion...and let it out.

It's a lot.

Permission to
Question

Like so many of the permissions you are invited to give, get, and take, this one can disrupt the status quo and tip you out of your comfort zone. That is why you may need permission to question. When we are comfortable, we tend not to ask questions. We might not worry where the benefits we are enjoying came from, if there were any negative consequences, or even if there might be a more innovative, expedient, or inclusive way to achieve the same results.

Questions are the antidote to comfort and complacency.

Questions keep us engaged, keep our minds and hearts open, and keep us moving toward a more positive future. Ask away! You have permission.

Permission to
Question

Encourage Inquiry

The most powerful way you can give this permission is to encourage and model inquiry yourself. Even on the homestretch toward implementation of your big project, continue to inquire and remain open to new discoveries. Inquire about what is working; inquire about the source of challenges and obstacles; inquire about what you are discovering about yourself and your team; inquire about the new insights, knowledge networks, and innovations that are emerging. Inquire and the whole world will inquire with you.

Challenge Assumptions

Many a business plan, marketing strategy, and product launch are built on faulty assumptions. The challenge with challenging assumptions is to become aware of those assumptions in the first place. Often we can't see the most obvious assumptions we make each day. Take the time and give yourself and your colleagues permission to surface and challenge assumptions early and often. What assumptions are you making about your employees? Your customers' needs? The market? Your supply chain? Your investors? The political climate? Your resources? Your brother-in-law's willingness to offer pro bono legal services? Okay, that last one may be a stretch, but you get the idea. *You can never ask too many questions or question too many assumptions.*

Milk Those Sacred Cows

Poor sweet cows. They never did anything to us. Yet we have assigned them responsibility for our most cherished projects, policies, and ideas. Giving permission to question means questioning even the things that are off-limits for questioning. Rather than idolize these as sacred, question how they achieved this status in the first place. Make friends with the cow and you may learn some important lessons. Which aspects of the cow do you want to continue to worship, and which are worthy of reviewing and revising? In friendship and with a spirit of inquiry, you may discover that sometimes a cow is just a cow. Moooo!

Permission to
Ask For What
You Need

It is so simple. In fact, it couldn't be simpler. Just *ask*.

There are actually two parts to this permission. First, you must *know* what you need. To know what you need, you must be present enough to receive the messages letting you know that you have a need that requires addressing. Second, and this can be the hard part, *ask* for what you need. Just ask. This can be especially hard if you were socialized that it was impolite to ask, or that only weak people have needs, or that you should be able to take care of all of your needs without asking for anything. We'd like to save you from a big investment in counseling and tell you that it's time to move on from all of that and start getting what you need. No one can partner with you to get those needs met if you don't ask.

Here are just a few things we would like to give you permission to ask for—and this is just for starters:

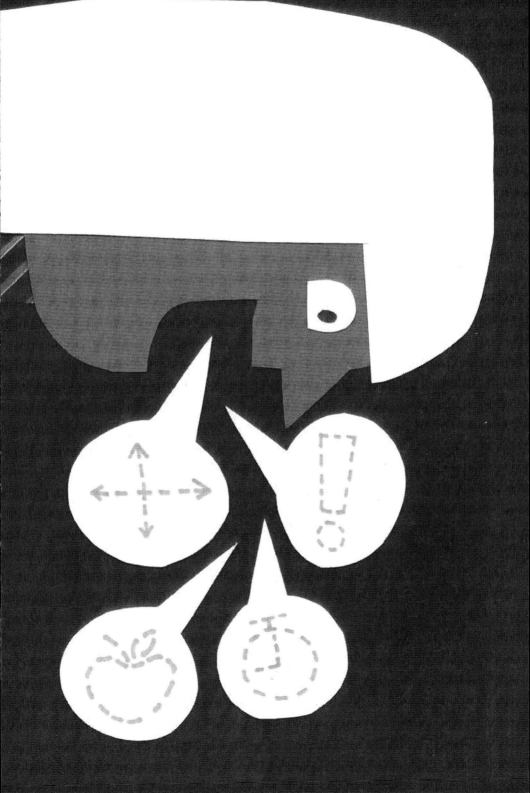

Permission to
Ask For What You Need

Help

Perhaps the most obvious, asking for help, is often the last one that occurs to us. Contrary to popular belief, you really don't have to do it all yourself. Has  the project expanded beyond your capacity? Is the deadline looming? Is your best friend getting married? Are you caring for an ill family member? ASK FOR HELP. You will be surprised how much is available to you. And the earlier you ask, the better. So ask early, ask often.

Time

Few of us feel like we have enough of it. Even fewer of us give ourselves permission to ask for more of it—especially more of it for ourselves. Ask for time. Time to be quiet, take a break, take a class, take a walk, get a massage; ask for time to talk, think, and/or tinker. Only you can ask for it.

Space

Asking for time is sometimes really a request for space. We all need it. Space is the breathing room that delivers us back into our lives, our natural energy, and sense of well-being. Sometimes we need physical space—a room of our own, a view of the water, a walk in the park. Sometimes we need mental, psychic, emotional, and spiritual space to simply be simple; we need space to space out. Everyone needs it. Few of us get enough of it, unless we give ourselves permission to ask for it.

Snacks

While he didn't explicitly mention it, snacks are at the foundational level of Maslow's hierarchy of needs. If your blood sugar is dropping, you cannot possibly take care of any of your other needs, let alone be a delightful, creative contributor. Give

yourself permission to ask for snacks. A healthy, nutritious, fresh boost of energy will restore you to your formerly friendly self and make everyone around you breathe a sigh of relief. Don't forget to share.

Permission to
Be Enthusiastic

Enthusiasm means to be filled with spirit. In an age of cynicism it is easy to be suspicious of unbridled enthusiasm. "What are they trying to sell me?" you may wonder. True enthusiasm has no external goal. It does not need to convince or cajole, because it springs from pure excitement about an idea, experience, or emerging possibility. Don't let the cynics in your world tempt you to hide your own enthusiasm. Let yourself be filled with as much spirit as you can stand.

Are you honestly excited about the new change strategy? The article or book you are reading? The new finance guy? Share your enthusiasm. You may unleash more energy than you knew existed by giving and taking this permission.

As it turns out, you are not too cool for school (and neither is anyone else)!

Permission to
Be Enthusiastic

Geek Out

Not all enthusiasm looks like standing up on your office chair waving your arms in excitement. Sometimes it looks like burying your head in the latest issue of *Popular Mechanics*, or spending hours experimenting with your new set of markers, or studying tomato plant genetics. It doesn't matter the topic; what matters is that you give yourself permission to immerse yourself deeply for the pure pleasure of it.

Cheerlead

One of the best ways to give this permission is to notice a spark of enthusiasm in someone else and cheer them on. Fan the flame of their fledgling idea, new curiosity, or interest. Cheerleaders help the home team stay in the game even when their energy is flagging, and they help the players see the value and possibilities even when they can't.

Recruit Your Own Cheering Squad

Hold a pep rally in your honor and invite your most positive friends and colleagues. Ask them for what you need: some positive feedback, some wind in your sails, some encouragement. You will find your own enthusiasm restored as you see it mirrored back to you. Rah! Rah! Sis boom bah!

Permission to
Be Quiet

Telling someone to "be quiet!" is not at all the same as giving them or yourself *permission* to be quiet. Perhaps it is because many of us grew up being told the former that we have some trouble with the latter. Unlike the stern directive, permission to be quiet is for the benefit of the quiet person, not the people around him or her.

In many contexts the quiet person is not valued (or at least noticed) as much as the noisy, busy, talkative person. We can be fooled into thinking that the noisy person is accomplishing something when, in fact, it is often in quiet that we accomplish the most. Give yourself permission to settle down, quiet down, and just be with and in the stillness. You may be amazed at how much you get done!

Permission to
Be Quiet

Shut Your Pie Hole

This image makes us smile, and we hope it helps you think about being quiet with a sense of humor. Whatever it brings to mind, if it encourages you to stop for a moment and simply shut it, you will begin to enjoy the benefits of quiet. You can't enjoy those benefits unless you, well...just plain stop talking. Make the conscious choice and effort to stop articulating, gesticulating, and blathering. It may take some doing at first but (trust us on this one) you and your colleagues will thank us later.

Notice

You don't need to do a thing in your quiet. In fact, the whole point is to enjoy the simplicity of your own being. In this simplicity, chances are you will start to notice. You may notice what you are experiencing and feeling, you may notice your surroundings, the scents, sights, and sounds that are only a backdrop when you are noisy. Notice what you notice in your quiet. It may be important.

Reflect

We repeat: You don't need to do a thing in your quiet. Though it is quite natural to have thoughts. So rarely do we consciously slow down and claim the time and space to be quiet, that when we do, thoughts and reflections flood in. Without *trying* to reflect, in your quiet you can simply be aware of your reflections. Notice the insights and connections your brain is making and processing. Relax and enjoy the movie of your thoughts, the soundtrack in your head, or maybe just the comfortable reclining seat itself. You may see some new dimension of yourself in the reflection, have a breakthrough idea, or simply enjoy being quiet.

Permission to Bring Your Whole Self

Organizations are no more machines than are individual people cogs in them. Despite our focus on measurable outcomes, productivity, efficiency, and profitability, organizations function best when seen as whole dynamic systems in a constant state of change. Whole systems require whole people.

When you give yourself and others permission to bring their whole selves to work, you allow space for all of the contexts in which people make meaning of their lives and work—home, family, hobbies, talents, and community to name a few. Our whole self also includes our lived experience in the moment (the degree to which we feel engaged, uncomfortable, enthusiastic) and the things that might be enabling or *dis*abling our ability to engage at the top of our capacity. When there is room to bring our whole selves (yes, even our silly selves) to work, the chances that we will feel seen, heard, appreciated, included, and engaged greatly increase.

Permission to
Bring Your
Whole Self

Check In

Never underestimate the value of simply taking a moment to "check in." Before you dive into the task at hand with your colleagues, or launch your idea generation session, give yourself and others permission to take a moment to check in. A few words about what is going on in your life, what you are feeling, your current relationship to the project at hand, etc. will greatly enhance the degree to which you and everyone else are actually "in the room" and present for the opportunities at hand. Checking in also ensures that no one has "checked out" before you have even begun!

Come Out

The GLBT community no longer has a corner on the market for coming out. In fact, coming out has always been about "coming in" to our whole selves and being willing to share more of our humanity with our fellow travelers. Are you a closet stamp collector? Avid gardener? Weekend paintball warrior? Abstract artist? Cyclist? Tutor? You may be surprised how much more people appreciate you when they see you as a whole human being and are invited to celebrate your enthusiasm with you. Who knows? You might give others permission to come out a little more, too!

Be Real

Nothing builds connection like showing up as your whole, un-airbrushed self. After years of polishing our personal brands, many of us have settled into the much easier and more enjoyable endeavor of just being ourselves—whomever that happens to be in any given moment or context. Presence, humanity, and mutual respect are the most compelling gifts you can offer to your colleagues and are most likely to encourage them to show up with their whole real selves, as well.

Permission to
Draw It

We began our lives ready to scribble, draw, and color with our crayons. We were all artists in our smocks made from Dad's shirt worn backwards. We could draw anything, and not even walls were safe from our power. As we grew older, we boxed up our crayons when we were told we couldn't draw something right or told ourselves we weren't artists. When we stopped drawing we lost a powerful tool to express ourselves, to gain a new perspective, to make the intangible tangible. We lost an important way of thinking. We lost an ally.

Drawing wants to be your friend again. Drawing wants to be appreciated for more than portraits and still lifes. She has many other abilities. Drawing can help you think through your ideas, help you communicate, and help you solve problems. In other words, drawing can also help you collaborate, cogitate, and incubate.

All we are saying is give drawing a chance.

Permission to
Draw It

Make a Mark for Yourself

It's time to move beyond our conceptions of drawing as the refined, finished museum pieces in gilded frames. These associations distract from drawing as a powerful practice and process, completely separate from a product. Make marks for yourself, and only for yourself. Give yourself permission to make messy drawings that are never finished. Make drawings that no one ever sees. When you make your mark(s) for yourself, you release the labels of Artist, Art, Viewer and let drawings (and all of the ideas, emotions, and insights that come with them) flow.

Get It on Paper

A piece of paper and a pen have magical powers. Ponder a problem you have. Pick up a pen and start writing and drawing it out on a piece of paper. Abracadabra! You can now see your conundrum from a new perspective. You have made it tangible, movable, and more understandable. A simple unlined piece of paper can reflect and clarify complexity. Magically you start to see how the parts connect to the whole—that there *is* a whole. Grab a piece of paper and (poof!) materialize it.

Build the Big Picture Together

Give a group of people a giant whiteboard and markers and soon they will create maps to whole new territories. It's so simple: just hang a giant sheet of paper on the wall (or paint a wall with chalkboard paint). Give every person the right tools and permission to draw. It's content that matters, not style. With the permission, environment, and resources to draw and think collaboratively, your team will soon be sailing off to new vistas they never could have imagined.

Permission to Connect

One of the best things about being human is our need and ability to make sense of the world and to know ourselves through connection. Our brains are meaning-making organs. Stare at any two unrelated objects, or watch any two people, and you will, unprompted, begin to tell yourself the story of their relationship. Far too often this wonderful human quest for connection and meaning is characterized as soft, subjective, emotional, and even a distraction from the practical concerns of business. Quite the opposite is true. Our need to connect and make connections is at the heart of our personal and shared success. Through connections we build the social ties that provide support. Through connections we also relate familiar ideas to each other to form new breakthrough ones.

Permission to
Connect

Relate

It's long been said that *who* you know is more important than *what* you know. It's true: The most successful people in any organization are the connectors, networkers, and even the socializers. Their success goes beyond simply *who* they know. Their willingness to truly relate to their fellow human beings is the key.

Relating is showing up to *their* whole self with your whole self.

Take this permission every day and you will enjoy the trust, mutual support, and well-being (and, yes, the occasional disappointment, frustration, and grief) that comes with being "related" to your fellow humans.

Link

There may not be anything new under the sun, but there are always new connections to make. There are new links to be made between ideas, images, disciplines, objects, ingredients, cultures, technologies, and more. Give yourself permission to explore beyond your familiar territory. Attend a conference in a new field, try reading journals, trade and popular magazines no one else in your area reads (*Dairy Goat Journal*, anyone?). Find out what is emerging in other industries and disciplines. Play around with the connections, links, and relationships to your field. What new questions are inspired? What new approaches can you envision? What talent or technologies might you borrow? To link is human.

Permission to
Include

Exclusion has its rewards. It can come with control, even a bit of power—at least temporarily. Inclusion, however, has even more to offer and comes with true power: staying power. Inclusion creates community and builds connections, communication, and trust. So, while inclusion may come at the expense of some control, the returns in overall engagement and creativity will make you wonder why you even worried about who or what to let in in the first place.

Bottom Line: Inclusion fosters belonging. Belonging fosters commitment, a willingness to persevere for the good of the team. Permission to include is also permission to trust the inherent good of the group and to trust that with more inclusion, the good of the group will flourish.

Permission to
Include

Include Information

It takes a lot of energy to control information. While information constraints may deliver some short-term gain for a chosen few, it sucks a lot of life out of the entire system. Rather than waste energy controlling information that everyone could benefit from, put energy into sharing responsibility for the information. Budget numbers not where they should be? How can everyone contribute to turn them around? Morale low in the marketing department? How can you harness the great energy in the finance department for their benefit? Design flaw in the new product about to launch? What solutions might your customers have? When the information is transparent to all, the likelihood that someone will see an innovative way forward radically increases.

Include People

Uck. There may be no worse feeling than the feeling of being left out. It conjures our worst memories of grade school oversights. Why stir all of that back up? Why not just include people this time around? Include interested parties. Include those affected by the new initiative or policy. Include those who will have to actually implement the change. Include those who are not normally included. Not only will you have more insight, you will create room for others to co-own the opportunity at hand.

AND if you are one of the people who sometimes gets excluded and think your invitation got lost in the mail, take permission to *include yourself!*

Include Perspectives

Including people, especially people who don't look, sound, and see exactly like you, means including more perspectives. If you really want people to feel good about where they are going, give them permission to be seen and heard. The inclusion of diverse perspectives provokes more and new thinking, and new ways of seeing. It also creates space for everyone. The point is not to implement every perspective; the point is to be sure as many as possible are included and respected. Come to think of it, through inclusion, you might just change the world.

Permission to Play

If there is any tragedy of adulthood, it is that many of us lost our fundamental, intrinsic delight in play. As we moved further and further into the commitments and routines of our responsible lives, play became something for the spaces in between and outside of our other commitments. Except for a lucky few, most of us entered lives in which work and play were not compatible. We got hooked into the dichotomy: work is serious, purposeful, and directed; play is silly, purposeless, and undirected.

It's now time to drop all of that nonsense and reclaim play as essential to your success and happiness.

Play can be an energizing diversion from routine, a warm-up for creative collaboration, and the attitude that infuses your entire approach. Think about it. What if you could make room for both work and play in the same experience? What if your work life could be as energizing as your play life? What might that look like? Feel like?

Permission to Play

Speak the Language of Play

Language has a big impact on reality. Notice what happens when you start talking about "playing with ideas," "making your workplace more of a playspace," giving people opportunities to "play new roles," and creating more "play in the system" to respond to change and opportunities. Start speaking the language of play and give yourself permission to live into your words.

Make Time to Play

Speaking the language of play can help break down the work-play dualism. So can giving yourself and your crew permission to take regular play breaks. A few minutes of Nerf basketball, Wii bowling, or a rousing improv game will bring you back to life and bring more life back to the project, meeting, and/or issue in front of you.

Make Space to Play

One of the best ways to give others permission to play is to bring some play into your space. Is your space conducive to playing with ideas and for people to play new roles? Is there space to collaborate, to gather informally, and to improvise and ideate? Does your space provoke new thinking, or does it emphasize order and routine? If you truly value the benefits of play, then be sure to give yourself and others permission to make space for it to happen.

Make Playspace

The space to play is much more than the physical setting. It is the space you co-create with your fellow player in each conversation and collaboration. Playspace is the space within and between people that provides the right mix of safety, provocation, presence, and generativity. Take responsibility for cultivating these dynamics and watch the play begin!

Permission to
Practice

Practice needs a new PR agent. Practice has been misrepresented as laborious, a necessary evil and, for those who are truly committed, even as the way to Carnegie Hall. The real value of practice is not as a means to a glorified end, it is in the practice itself. Give yourself permission to surrender to *a* practice, any practice. All that is important is that it is *your* practice. Yoga, daily writing, watercolor painting, the cello, computer programming, it matters not. The opportunity is in the practice.

Shift your relationship from an attachment to the outcome of practice, to immersion in the practice itself. Enjoy all of that extra available energy that has been released with that attachment—all the more for your practice!

Permission to
Practice

Do the Time

Whether your practice is tennis or calligraphy, you have to do the time. You may do your time on the court, or at your writing desk, or any other appropriate setting; the point is to honor yourself and your practice enough to devote consistent time to it. Practice before the noise of your day invades or practice once it has started to quiet down; take a break to practice or *make* a break to practice. Just do the time.

Practice for the Practice.

Perfection is not the goal of practice; the practice itself is the goal. Find the joy in the practice. Take permission to surrender to the fullness of doing and being your practice. Practice for presence.

It's All Practice

Theater and life are full of performances. Whether we want our performances reviewed or not, they will be. Yet every performance is also another opportunity to practice—to practice interviewing, auditioning, presenting, collaborating, selling, creating, writing, thinking on your feet, managing, and organizing. It's all practice.

Permission to Celebrate!

It is all-too-easy to motor along at work focusing only on the outcomes and quickly moving on to the next pressing deadline, meeting, or project without taking the time to celebrate the accomplishments, new learning, and relationships along the way.

This soon takes its toll.

The good news is that acknowledgement, appreciation, and recognition consistently rank high on employee satisfaction surveys and indicators of great places to work. So why not take a moment to stop and smell the roses (or birthday cake) and spread the good will, appreciation, and happiness around?

Celebrations can be formal and ritualized, or informal and spontaneous, as well as public or private. The best forms of celebration often cost little or nothing.

Permission to
Celebrate!

Throw Your Own Party (and toot your own noise maker)

We've been well socialized to be humble about our own successes (and, in turn, stingy with ourselves). However, there is nothing stingy about sharing those successes with others and using them as an opportunity to spread the good energy around! Throwing your own party is also a great opportunity to share the glory with others.

Celebrate Along the Way

So many of our projects are long and complex with no clear beginning, middle, or end. It is important to acknowledge the successes along the way. Together with your more tangible benchmarks, don't forget to celebrate new learning, insight, and exposure, as well as resource-sharing and new collaborative relationships.

Just Say It

Often the informal, spontaneous acknowledgements are the best. If you don't "just say it" in the moment, you may miss the perfect chance to celebrate your colleagues and your shared successes. Hooray for everyone!

Permission to Immerse Yourself

The best way to learn a new language is to immerse yourself in it. A relatively short time living, breathing, eating, sleeping, and (if you are lucky) even dreaming the language, its people, and their culture will do more for you than years of study. The same is true for every area worthy of our passion and curiosity. Though we know its value, immersion is a gift that we rarely give ourselves. There are so many distractions and excuses for not surrendering our whole being to a single exploration.

Our lives are not likely to get simpler. Here-in lies the opportunity! Rather than lament lack of possibility for new learning and deep experience, we can get creative and imagine *how* we can immerse ourselves in our passions without completely dropping out of the rest of our lives. You can immerse yourself for a moment, an afternoon, or a full-blown sabbatical. The amount of time is not the issue, it is your willingness to allow yourself the fullness of experience in the time you have.

Permission to
Immerse Yourself

Dive In

When it comes to immersion, you are either in or you're out. You are either standing at the side of the pool with your toes curled on the edge or you are completely immersed in the pool. The difference between these two states of being is the leap itself. Take it. Give yourself permission to dive into the pool of your new idea, venture, learning opportunity, job, relationship, and life itself!

Feel It

Surrendering to immersion can open up all of the other wonderful ways we can experience the world and ourselves—intuitively, emotionally, relationally, spiritually, and somatically, with our whole body and senses. Some even become open to ecological experience as part of something much greater than themselves. Through immersion we can feel in ways we never before imagined. What inspiration and creativity is available to you now?

Drop Out

Some immersions really do need your full attention for an extended amount of time. This may be the biggest permission (and gift) you can give yourself. Dropping out of your regularly scheduled life for immersion is really about dropping *in* to yourself. Always wanted to go work on that volunteer project, apply for the grant for the artist's retreat? Maybe it's finally time to take your friend up on her invitation to stay in the empty coach house to finish your novel.

Leave your distractions (and cell phone) behind and immerse yourself.

Permission to
Make a Mess

Life is messy. Beautifully, perfectly messy.

Messiness is simply part of the process of life and a natural dimension of change. When we allow people, relationships, collaborations, and the creative process to have their own innate messiness, we become *part* of the process, rather than outside of it. When we allow ourselves, others, and the co-creative process of organizational life to have our/their own messiness, we reap previously unimagined benefits. These gifts include new energy, stress relief, creative insight and, very often, the unexpected discovery of the organic efficiencies of people and processes, as well!

Permission to
Make a Mess

Appreciate the Mess

On the other side of our mess-aversion, are some pretty wonderful opportunities. Many breakthrough innovations have come from messes: experiments gone awry, previously unnoticed phenomenon, un-appreciated talent in emerging art forms, to name only a few. Learn the lessons of the mess. Yes, sometimes it is telling you that you've made a wrong turn; just as often there are possibilities in the unexpected. Beyond new discoveries and insights, there is the value of simply allowing the life process to have some room to emerge.

Get Your Hands Dirty

Part of the challenge of appreciating the value of the mess is that most of us have been well socialized to clean up our messes as quickly as possible and (better yet) avoid them at all costs. Most kids (and gardeners) know the fun of plunging into the mess with both hands. Be part of it. Enjoy the visceral pleasure of dirt underneath your fingernails, even if just for an hour or so. A little soap and water will wash the mess away, but not the lived experience, joy, and discoveries you made in it.

Break It

That old saying, "If it ain't broke,..." is rooted in a human need for comfort and routine. It is *not* the hallmark of creative, engaged people, let alone innovating organizations. Engaged, playful, curious, creative people break things all the time; they make messes every day to see what's inside, and to start over—simply because it's fun. Look around and find your favorite metaphorical Ming vase and see what happens when you break it!

Permission to
Take a Risk

Risks are risky. At least they seem that way—especially in the middle of the night, as we stare wide-eyed at the ceiling imagining all that could go wrong, all of the horrible "what ifs." These shadows only masquerade as dream-eating monsters; they are, in fact, only our fears sent by our human need for comfort and consistency.

The risk is often to our illusion of security. We may believe we are secure when we have reached a magic number in our bank account, or when we find our perfect mate, or settle into a good job. All of these are wonderful comforts and, in reality, all provide only the illusion of security. Life is change. No matter the degree of security we believe we have achieved, we are sure to experience upheaval to shake us out of both comfortable and uncomfortable times. Protecting comfort at all costs can well mean just that—a very costly comfort, indeed.

Before you can take a risk, you must identify some good juicy risks to take. What risk would you take if you had no fear? If there were no obstacles? Just imagine.

Permission to
Take a Risk

Rehearse the Risk

Sometimes the fear of risk keeps us from even imagining the possibilities available to us. You can actually rehearse risk-taking from the safety of your favorite comfy chair. Imagine yourself at your most confident, filled with calm. Imagine what costume you will wear, the roles other players will play. Imagine the enthusiastic response of the audience. Rehearse and then when it is time, play your part with all of the presence of the first time. You are ready for this performance.

Risk Big

There are times in life when we are invited to take an apparently big risk: leave a comfortable, but unrewarding job, take on a new challenge that will stretch us more than we have ever stretched, dive into a completely new context or culture, leaving behind all that was familiar. These risks come with great reward and very real losses. If you are holding back simply because you fear the unknown, there's a good chance this risk has your name on it. Take it.

Risk Small

Most of the risks we encounter are everyday garden-variety risks. These tend to be of the emotional/psychological type. They actually don't seem so small in the moment or when you contemplate them in the dark of night; they can seem just as ominous as any other risk. Perhaps you are considering risking telling the truth, *your* truth: coming out about how you really feel, saying what you mean, asking for what you want and need; or risking sharing your new idea, challenging the way things have always been done around here; or standing up for what you believe in or taking a new creative risk. These risks can come with even greater reward—deliverance into your whole self. The possible loss of your former, less-integrated self and the loss of the status quo are nothing in comparison to what you stand to gain.

Permission to
Walk Away

Sometimes our virtues can be our biggest enemy. Commitment, loyalty, perseverance, and plain old stick-to-itiveness are all wonderful qualities. Like most of our blessings, they can be our curse. When our commitment to hang in there overshadows the bold-faced writing on the wall that this endeavor, project, job, or relationship is simply not working, or at least not for you, it is time to give yourself permission to walk away.

Walking away may at first appear to contradict every value you hold near and dear, but it is not. Walking away is grounded in the same values, just applied to yourself! Walking away is *commitment* to your own well-being, *loyalty* to your own vision, *perseverance* in your passion, and *stick-to-itiveness* to your own hopes and dreams.

Permission to Walk Away

Jump Out of the Pot

As the analogy goes, sometimes we don't realize just how unmanageable a situation has become because the temperature in our lobster pot has gone up in imperceptible increments. Rather than wait for things to come to a full boil, attune yourself to the conditions and know your limits. This way you can jump out of the pot while the jumping is still good. Then just keep on walking.

Take a Break

Not all walk-aways need to be permanent. You can walk away for an hour, an afternoon, a few months, even longer. The reality is, nothing is permanent. If your resistance is to the "foreverness" of your walk, give yourself permission to simply take a break. Chances are good that while you are out strolling, you will discover more about yourself and the possibilities/limitations of your situation that will give you new perspective and energy when you return.

Let It Go

Attachment is the biggest obstacle to growth. We get attached to things as they are: to our co-workers and to that cute little café down the street with the killer brownies. We also get attached to situations that may no longer be giving us life, offering us new learning and growth. It may take some doing, some soul-searching, and some support to recognize that now is the time to simply release it. Loosen your grip on what you thought would be and acknowledge what is.

Let.   It.   Go.

Permission to Improvise

Many years ago people thought they should only have to improvise at work if they failed to plan well enough. It turns out it is impossible to have enough plans to account for all possible unexpected occurrences. Thankfully we have begun to learn a few lessons from those who create entire evenings of entertainment live on stage. Musicians, actors, and dancers are just a few artists who embrace the unexpected, rather than brace for it.

Rather than run from your next opportunity for spontaneous action, run headlong into this chance to surprise yourself and your fellow players with what you co-create on the spot.

Permission to
Improvise

Develop Your Improv Competence

The good news is that there are actually principles and skills you can learn to enhance your ability to respond to the unexpected and unplanned. For starters, you can learn how to say, "Yes, and..." (build on your partner's idea, rather than shooting down with "yeah, but..."); you can learn how to make your partner, team, or organization look good and how to offer the best "gifts" possible to enhance the success of the improvisation. Opportunities to develop your competence abound through local classes or inviting an improvisation expert to your organization. Stumped for ideas? Call us.

Raise Your Improv Consciousness

Improvisation consciousness is the heightened state of awareness that comes from full engagement in the present moment. Improvisers are not making their weekend plans or worrying about their e-mail box when they are co-creating on the spot. They are drawing on all available resources to respond to the opportunity before them. Notice your state of awareness and engagement the next time you are called to improvise. Give yourself permission to cultivate that awareness more frequently and see what additional creative spaces open up.

Build Your Improv Confidence

Very likely you came into the world with full-blown confidence in your ability to improvise—to create a fort from a sheet and the kitchen table and entire worlds from a pile of sand. While you may have lost your confidence over time, you can get it back. Make time for improvised play throughout your week and soon you will feel that familiar improvisation confidence return. Look out, sandbox!

Permission to Say "I Don't Know"

You likely have made your way in the world, in part, by being acknowledged for your rich knowledge and experience. Jobs are won and lost based on expertise, among other things, and credibility is often built or diminished based on the perception of what we know or can do.

It is risky, then, to admit that we don't know. This is not the preferred state for many of us well socialized to value order, control, and predictability. However, not knowing can actually open up vast new possibilities for exploration and insight, not to mention collaboration and co-creation. When we co-create the space in which it is safe enough to say "I don't know," we also create space for new learning and for others to drop their defenses. When we lighten up on our well-polished professional identities, we also become open to the exciting prospect of new discoveries, perspectives, and ways of thinking and being!

Saying "I don't know" also makes room for more than one right answer and to acknowledge and hold a bit of complexity, uncertainty, and, yes, discomfort.

Permission to
Say "I Don't Know"

Be a Beginner

The greatest learning and discovery opportunities are at the beginning. What if you let go of all of your years of experience, training, and expertise and allowed yourself to explore as if you truly didn't know? What might you discover? What room might you make for others to discover?

Know You Don't Know What You Don't Know

The vexing reality of new learning and engagement is that we are often limited from discovering more by what we already know. When we turn the tables on our expertise and acknowledge that there is much we don't know, we have permission to re-engage for new learning.

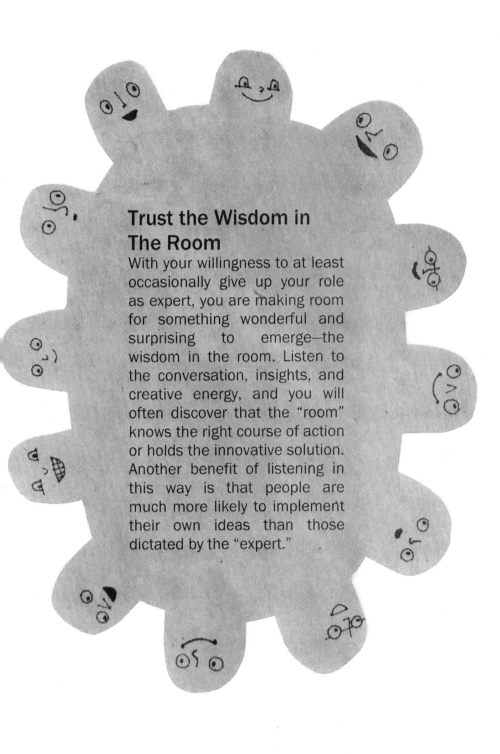

Trust the Wisdom in The Room

With your willingness to at least occasionally give up your role as expert, you are making room for something wonderful and surprising to emerge—the wisdom in the room. Listen to the conversation, insights, and creative energy, and you will often discover that the "room" knows the right course of action or holds the innovative solution. Another benefit of listening in this way is that people are much more likely to implement their own ideas than those dictated by the "expert."

Permission to
Rest

Ahhhh...rest. It refreshes and restores. Rests are not just for when we are tired. Rests are the pauses in the music that allow us to take in all that has gone before, for excitement to build, and for possibility to rush in. In a culture where time and money are considered one and the same, rest is worth every penny. When we return from a rest, momentary or lengthy, we bring new energy, perspective, enthusiasm, and focus. In fact, often we make up any time spent resting with our new energy and focus!

Permission to
Rest

Be a Sloth

Somewhere along the way, sloths got a bad rap. Have you ever actually watched a sloth? Even when they are awake (which is rare) they move verrrrry slowly. The interesting thing is that even watching a sloth for a few minutes may cause your own breathing to start to slow and perhaps a little grin to creep across your face. None of us can keep up the same high pace day in and day out. Take a lesson from the sweet sloth and see what happens if you slow down a bit and act as if there is no stress in your life. How restful!

Recharge

Resting is, of course, a great way to recharge. And recharging is a great way to rest! In an open system everything eventually loses energy. Physics tells us that the energy isn't lost forever; it has just gone somewhere else. But where did it go and how to get it back? Here's a place to start: Think about what energizes you. Lunch with a friend who makes you laugh? Yoga class? Collaborating with imaginative colleagues? Taking a walk through the park? Salsa dancing? A weekday matinee? A meditation break? The possibilities are endless. The trick is knowing when you need to recharge and having a boatload of options to choose from when you need a boost.

Make it a Routine

Our bodies *love* routine! They love regular (healthy) meals, regular exercise, and yes, regular rest. Even if your life defies anything resembling habits, you may be surprised at the degree of power you have to claim a few sacred spaces. With a few boundaries set for yourself—times for resting and exercising, time with family and friends—you will discover that you have more energy than ever to be productive and creative within the remaining time. You may also discover another side benefit: your family, friends, and colleagues might respect you even more for staking some claims and even take permission to create some sacred routines for themselves!

Permission to Wonder

The demands of work life can make us susceptible to the tyranny of the task. In our race to meet deadlines, be productive and efficient, most of us rarely give ourselves permission to push back from our desk, stare out the window, and simply wonder. We can wonder alone or in groups, over the course of a few minutes or days or weeks. The point is to invite generative, curious, questioning, life-giving possibilities into the mix. From what we can tell, wondering is a uniquely human capacity. Use it!

Permission to
Wonder

Remember the Magic

When was the last time you truly experienced "awe"? Perhaps it was at the rim of the Grand Canyon or another of the Seven Wonders of the World. The experience of true awe is all-encompassing. This is why magic shows, fantasy, and wizardry are so compelling when we allow our childlike innocence to breathe. Magic allows us to wonder with our whole being. If it's been awhile since you experienced it, make a concerted effort to experience something genuinely *awesome*. Imagine the possibilities when we allow ourselves such permission!

Be Curious

Rather than motor past the metaphorical roadside attractions announcing the "world's largest ball of twine" or "tiniest church," allow yourself a bit of childlike wonder and take the unplanned detour. It might attune you to other surprises on your drive and restore your natural curiosity about the delightful quirks in the people, places, and phenomena that surround you every day.

Ask "What If?"

A common creativity technique is to play around with wild variations of the opportunity at hand by way of "what if" questions. "What if all of our customers worked in our building? Lived in our community? Were our neighbors?" "What if we could send holographic versions of ourselves to conferences?" "What if none of our employees had to work for a living?" "What if we achieved the central goal of our mission?" Even taking the time to brainstorm "what if" questions alone will begin to open up brain cells and invite engagement you didn't know you had.

What would it be like if what *could* be *was*? With a little wondering, you may discover it is not so far off as you thought.

Permission to
Provoke

We all need to have our comfort disrupted from time to time—to be taken on a Jacob Marley journey through the world from other people's perspectives, to be provoked out of our routine ways of doing and seeing. We also may be called to step into the role of the provocateur. While it may not be a comfortable role to play, it is often the most valuable. Give yourself and your pals permission to provoke each other out of your comfort zones.

Before long, you might even get more comfortable with discomfort and notice people are not spending quite so much energy protecting their familiar ways of thinking, doing, and being, but giving themselves permission to provoke themselves!

Permission to
Provoke

Rock the Boat

Everyone knows what happens to the person who rocks the boat. At best they get a strong dose of dirty looks, at worst, they get pitched overboard. Who wants to be *that* person? The answer is anyone who wants to work at the top of their talent and bring out the best in others. The first few waves will be a bit disorienting (as they should be). As people get their sea legs, they will start rocking and rolling with the new flow. With this new-found agility, provocations become welcome disruptions that help keep ideas and energy flowing.

Stir the Pot

All pots need a bit of stirring before they make it to the table. Stirring the pot is when the good stuff happens. Unexpected flavors co-mingle to create new surprises, liquids thicken, and contents recombine into whole new flavors. Stir the pot and ring the dinner bell!

Poke

Way more fun than the button you can press on Facebook, poking someone in real life has context and a bit of provocative content as well. You might poke someone by leaving a book or article on their desk, sending a friendly disruptive e-mail, or otherwise poking them just enough to shake them out of their comfortable routine. Very likely the "pokee" will welcome the disruption and circle back to you with the ideas you set in motion. Even better, the pokee might be provoked to become a poker and before you know it, you will have unleashed a tidal wave of provocation!

Permission to
Start Now

Sometimes we think we need permission from someone or something else to start. Once we have that additional degree or credential we will have permission. Once we have more experience we will have permission. Once we get the blessing of our parents, partner, or mentor we will have permission. Once we have more time, money, or real estate we will have permission. There are a million possible people and entities to assign this power to. The dirty secret is that this power is only an illusion, and the only way to start is by *taking* permission, and the only time to start is now.

Permission to
Start Now

Start Small

Your new endeavor, project, or commitment may appear overwhelming when taken as a whole. Changing your corporate culture, learning a new language, ending world hunger are all gigantic, worthy missions. Just thinking about them could make anyone want to go lie down. It is much more do-able to start small. Start by hosting a small lively lunch 'n' learn session, or signing up for a short-term beginning language class, or volunteering to serve meals to the homeless one night a week. Start small and start now.

Start Big

The best way to get into a body of water is to jump with both feet. Make a big, loud, sloppy splash. Once you are in it, you can figure out the rest. Many worthwhile actions are like this; there is no halfway, only full immersion. You may be surprised just how much capacity you have to thrive in this new situation, and very likely it's not nearly as deep as you thought.

Start Imperfectly

It is much better to start now than wait to have all of the fine details worked out. There will *always* be more details, and you couldn't have possibly planned for them all in advance. Perfection is the enemy of action. Start imperfectly, learn along the way, and have fun doing it!

Epilogue:
An Invitation

There is no one right way to give, get, or take permission. The permissions we have invited you to explore in this book are only intended to get you started. We fully expect that once you get going, you will discover many more permissions worth giving, getting and taking. Please consider sharing additional permissions you discover, or those you'd like us to write about next. We'd also love to hear what happens for you when you take up the invitation of permission. We are just getting started, ourselves!

We also invite you to give permission to others who could benefit from generating more ideas, being more of themselves and having more fun at work! We have some more playful ideas for people you might want to give permission to at **permissiongivers.com.**

The Co-Creators

Pamela Meyer loves collaborating with smart, creative, and playful people. She gets to do this through her work as president of Meyer Creativity Associates with organizations that want to create dynamic workspaces for innovating, learning, and changing. She also teaches and learns with inspiring adult graduate students who want to learn about organizational change and adult learning principles and practice at DePaul University's School for New Learning, where she is also director of the Center to Advance Education for Adults. Pamela has put in a bit of time in school herself, with a B.F.A. in theater and two master's degrees and a doctorate in Human and Organizational Systems.

If you like this book, you might also enjoy Pamela's other books, *From Workplace to Playspace: Innovating, Learning and Changing Through Dynamic Engagement* (Jossey-Bass, 2010) and *Quantum Creativity* (McGraw/Contemporary, 2000). Links to these and several other book chapters and articles by Pamela can be found on her website: www.meyercreativity.com.

Thanks, in part, to the wonderful time she had playing on this book, Pamela is giving herself permission to start skiing again.

Brandy Agerbeck is a lucky ladybug. She does her two favorite things for a living: thinking and drawing. As a graphic facilitator, she creates live, large-scale conceptual maps of conversations. These images help her clients navigate the  complex territory of their meetings, workshops, and conferences. Brandy loves getting clients' ideas out of their heads and onto paper – so they can see what the heck they are saying. She has been called a spatial superstar with her strength in seeing connections between thoughts and organizing them into the bigger picture. Since 1996, she has facilitated groups from two to one thousand across industries. She's been drawing since age two and is thankful her childhood love has become her livelihood, enabling people to do better work.

Brandy teaches people the power of graphic facilitation and how to use drawing as a thinking tool. Learn more at her site: www.Loosetooth.com.

Brandy's favorite permission is the one she and Pamela gave themselves to create this book.